HAMLET
Prince of Denmark

WILLIAM SHAKESPEARE'S
HAMLET
PRINCE OF DENMARK

ADAPTED FOR PERFORMANCE BY NICLAS OLSON

New Muses Theatre Company | Tacoma

Printed in the United States of America
First Edition, 2020

ISBN: 9798646460098

www.NiclasOlson.com

"Uneasy lies the head that wears a crown."
William Shakespeare, Henry IV Pt. 2

Production History

HAMLET, PRINCE OF DENMARK had its world premiere on January 11, 2019 at the Dukesbay Theater in Tacoma, in a production by New Muses Theatre Company. It was directed and designed by Niclas Olson. Costumes and sound were by Bethany Bevier. The board operator was Erinne Kellogg.

BERNARDO	Victoria Ashley
HORATIO	Mason Quinn
THE GHOST	Juan Aleman II
CLAUDIUS	Juan Aleman II
GERTRUDE	Dayna Childs
HAMLET	Niclas Olson
LAERTES	Xander Layden
OPHELIA	Cassie Jo Fastabend
POLONIUS	Angela Parisotto
ROSENCRANTZ	Victoria Ashley
GUILDENSTERN	Xander Layden
A GRAVEDIGGER	Angela Parisotto

Characters

HAMLET	Prince of Denmark
GERTRUDE	his mother, Queen of Denmark
CLAUDIUS	Hamlet's uncle, King of Denmark
POLONIUS	Claudius' Chief of Staff
OPHELIA	Polonius' daughter
LAERTES	a student, Polonius' son
HORATIO	a student
ROSENCRANTZ	an actor
GUILDENSTERN	an actor
BERNARDO	a soldier
THE GHOST	of Hamlet's father
A GRAVEDIGGER	

Setting

In and around the Palace of Elsinore, Denmark

HAMLET
Prince of Denmark

ACT ONE

SCENE ONE
the battlements

BARNARDO
>Who's there?

HORATIO
>Nay, answer me. Stand and unfold yourself.

BARNARDO
>Long live the King!

HORATIO
>Barnardo.

BARNARDO
>She.

HORATIO
>You come most carefully upon your hour.

BARNARDO
>'Tis now struck twelve. Is Horatio there?

HORATIO
>A piece of him.
>What, has this thing appeared again tonight?

BARNARDO
>I have seen nothing.

HORATIO
>Tush, tush, 'twill not appear.

The Ghost appears.

William Shakespeare

BARNARDO

Peace, break thee off! Look where it comes again.
In the same figure like the King that's dead.

HORATIO

What art thou that usurp'st this time of night,
Together with that fair and warlike form
In which the majesty of buried Denmark
Did sometimes march? By heav'n, I charge thee,
    speak.

BARNARDO

It is offended. See, it stalks away.

HORATIO

Stay! speak! speak! I charge thee, speak!

The Ghost disappears.

BARNARDO

How now, Horatio, you tremble and look pale.
Is not this something more than fantasy?
What think you on 't?

HORATIO

Before my God, I might not this believe
Without the sensible and true avouch
Of mine own eyes.

BARNARDO

                Is it not like the King?

HORATIO

As thou art to thyself.

                    HAMLET, PRINCE OF DENMARK

BARNARDO
> Thus twice before, and jump at this dead hour,
> With martial stalk hath he gone by our watch.

HORATIO
> This bodes some strange eruption to our state.
> A mote it is to trouble the mind's eye.
> *(the Ghost returns)*
> But soft, behold! Lo, where it comes again!
> I'll cross it though it blast me. - Stay, illusion!
> If thou hast any sound or use of voice,
> Speak to me. Stay and speak! - Stop it, Barnardo.

BARNARDO
> 'Tis here.

HORATIO
> 'Tis here.

The Ghost disappears

BARNARDO
> 'Tis gone.
> We do it wrong, being so majestical,
> To offer it the show of violence.

HORATIO
> It was about to speak when the cock crew.
> Break we our watch up, and by my advice
> Let us impart what we have seen tonight
> Unto young Hamlet; for, upon my life,
> This spirit, dumb to us, will speak to him.

SCENE TWO
the throne room

*Claudius before a large crowd. Gertrude
beside him. Hamlet watches from a
distance.*

CLAUDIUS
> Though yet of Hamlet our dear brother's death
> The memory be green, and that it us befitted
> To bear our hearts in grief, and our whole kingdom
> To be contracted in one brow of woe,
> Yet so far hath discretion fought with nature
> That we with wisest sorrow think on him
> Together with remembrance of ourselves.
> Therefore our sometime sister, now our queen,
> Have we (as 'twere with a defeated joy,
> With mirth in funeral and with dirge in marriage,
> In equal scale weighing delight and dole)
> Taken to wife. Nor have we herein barred
> Your better wisdoms, which have freely gone
> With this affair along. For all, our thanks.
>> *(descends the platform as the crowd
>> disperses)*
> But now, my cousin Hamlet and my son -

HAMLET
> (*aside*) A little more than kin and less than kind.

CLAUDIUS
> How is it that the clouds still hang on you?

HAMLET
> Not so, my lord; I am too much in the sun.

GERTRUDE

    Good Hamlet, cast thy nighted color off,
    And let thine eye look like a friend on Denmark.
    Do not forever with thy vailed lids
    Seek for thy noble father in the dust.
    Thou know'st 'tis common; all that lives must die,
    Passing through nature to eternity.

HAMLET

    Ay, madam, it is common.

GERTRUDE

                  If it be,
    Why seems it so particular with thee?

HAMLET

    "Seems," madam? Nay, it is. I know not "seems."
    'Tis not alone my inky cloak, good mother,
    Nor customary suits of solemn black,
    Together with all forms, moods, shapes of grief,
    That can denote me truly. These indeed "seem,"
    For they are actions that a man might play;
    But I have that within which passes show,
    These but the trappings and the suits of woe.

CLAUDIUS

    'Tis sweet and commendable in your nature,
      Hamlet,
    To give these mourning duties to your father.
    But you must know your father lost a father,
    That father lost, lost his, and the survivor bound
    In filial obligation for some term
    To do obsequious sorrow. But to persever
    In obstinate condolement is a course
    Of impious stubbornness. 'Tis unmanly grief.

Why should we in our peevish opposition
Take it to heart? Fie, 'tis a fault to heaven,
A fault against the dead, a fault to nature,
To reason most absurd, whose common theme
Is death of fathers, and who still hath cried,
From the first corse till he that died today,
"This must be so." We pray you, throw to earth
This unprevailing woe and think of us
As of a father; for let the world take note,
You are the most immediate to our throne,
And with no less nobility of love
Than that which dearest father bears his son
Do I impart toward you. For your intent
In going back to school in Wittenberg,
It is most retrograde to our desire,
And we beseech you, bend you to remain.

GERTRUDE

Let not thy mother lose her prayers, Hamlet.
I pray thee, stay with us. Go not to Wittenberg.

HAMLET

I shall in all my best obey you, madam.

CLAUDIUS

Why, 'tis a loving and a fair reply.
Be as ourself in Denmark. - Madam, come.
This gentle and unforced accord of Hamlet
Sits smiling to my heart. In grace, away.

*Exit Claudius and Gertrude. Hamlet is
alone.*

                    HAMLET, PRINCE OF DENMARK

HAMLET
O, that this too, too sullied flesh would melt,
Thaw, and resolve itself into a dew,
Or that the Everlasting had not fixed
His canon 'gainst self-slaughter! O God, God,
How weary, stale, flat, and unprofitable
Seem to me all the uses of this world!
Fie on 't. Fie! That it should come to this:
But two months dead--nay, not so much, not two.
So excellent a king. So loving to my mother
That he might not beteem the winds of heaven
Visit her face too roughly. Heaven and Earth,
Must I remember? Why, she would hang on him
As if increase of appetite had grown
By what it fed on. And yet, within a month
(Let me not think on 't; frailty, thy name is woman!),
A little month, or ere those shoes were old
With which she followed my poor father's body,
She, even she, married with my uncle,
My father's brother, but no more like my father
Than I to Hercules. Within a month,
Ere yet the salt of most unrighteous tears
Had left the flushing in her galled eyes,
She married. O, most wicked speed, to post
With such dexterity to incestuous sheets!
It is not, nor it cannot come to good.
But break, my heart, for I must hold my tongue.

Enter Horatio

HORATIO
Hail to your Lordship.

HAMLET
Horatio - or I do forget myself!

HORATIO
The same, my lord, and your poor servant ever.

HAMLET
Sir, my good friend. I'll change that name with you.
But what, in faith, make you from Wittenberg?

HORATIO
My lord, I came to see your father's funeral.

HAMLET
I prithee, do not mock me, fellow student.
I think it was to see my mother's wedding.

HORATIO
Indeed, my lord, it followed hard upon.

HAMLET
Thrift, thrift, Horatio. The funeral baked meats
Did coldly furnish forth the marriage tables.
My father... methinks I see my father.

HORATIO
Where, my lord?

HAMLET
                    In my mind's eye, Horatio.

HORATIO
My lord, I think I saw him yesternight.

HAMLET
Saw who?

                HAMLET, PRINCE OF DENMARK

HORATIO
     My lord, the King your father.

HAMLET
                                   The King my father?
     For God's love, let me hear!

HORATIO
     Two nights together had these gentlemen,
     In the dead waste and middle of the night,
     Been thus encountered: a figure like your father,
     Appears before them and with solemn march
     Goes slow and stately by them. This to me
     In dreadful secrecy impart they did,
     And I with them the third night kept the watch,
     Where, as they had delivered, both in time,
     The apparition comes. I knew your father;
     These hands are not more like.

HAMLET
                                   But where was this?

HORATIO
     My lord, upon the platform where we watch.

HAMLET
     Did you not speak to it?

HORATIO
                              My lord, I did,
     But answer made it none.

HAMLET
       '
                                   Tis very strange.

HORATIO
    As I do live, my honored lord, 'tis true.

HAMLET
    I would I had been there.

HORATIO
    It would have much amazed you.

HAMLET
    I will watch tonight.
    Perchance 'twill walk again.

HORATIO
                                    I warrant it will.

HAMLET
    If it assume my noble father's person,
    I'll speak to it, though hell itself should gape
    And bid me hold my peace. I pray you still,
    If you have hitherto concealed this sight,
    Let it be tenable in your silence still;
    And whatsomever else shall hap tonight,
    Give it an understanding but no tongue.
    Upon the platform, 'twixt eleven and twelve,
    I'll visit you.

HORATIO
            Our duty to your Honor.
        (exits)

HAMLET
    My father's spirit - in arms! All is not well.
    I doubt some foul play. Would the night were
        come!

Till then, sit still, my soul. Foul deeds will rise,
Though all the earth o'erwhelm them, to men's
eyes.

SCENE THREE
Polonius' house

LAERTES

> My necessaries are embarked. Farewell,
> But let me hear from you.

OPHELIA

> Do you doubt that?

LAERTES

> For Hamlet, and the trifling of his favor,
> Hold it a fashion and a toy in blood,
> A violet in the youth of primy nature,
> Forward, not permanent, sweet, not lasting,
> The perfume and suppliance of a minute,
> No more.

OPHELIA

> No more but so?

LAERTES

> Think it no more.
> His greatness weighed, his will is not his own,
> For he himself is subject to his birth.
> And therefore must his choice be circumscribed
> Unto the voice and yielding of that body
> Whereof he is the head. Then, if he says he loves
> you,
> It fits your wisdom so far to believe it
> As he in his particular act and place
> May give his saying deed, which is no further
> Than the main voice of Denmark goes withal.
> Then weigh what loss your honor may sustain
> If with too credent ear you list his songs

HAMLET, PRINCE OF DENMARK

Or lose your heart or your chaste treasure open
To his unmastered importunity.
Fear it, Ophelia; fear it, my dear sister,
And keep you in the rear of your affection,
Out of the shot and danger of desire.

OPHELIA

I shall the effect of this good lesson keep
As watchman to my heart.

LAERTES

O, fear me not.
(enter Polonius)
A double blessing is a double grace.
Occasion smiles upon a second leave.

POLONIUS

Yet here, Laertes? Aboard, aboard, for shame!
The wind sits in the shoulder of your sail,
And you are stayed for. There, my blessing with
thee.
Be thou familiar, but by no means vulgar.
Those friends thou hast, and their adoption tried,
Grapple them unto thy soul with hoops of steel,
But do not dull thy palm with entertainment
Of each new-hatched, unfledged courage. Beware
Of entrance to a quarrel, but, being in,
Bear 't that th' opposed may beware of thee.
Neither a borrower nor a lender be,
For loan oft loses both itself and friend.
This above all: to thine own self be true,
And it must follow, as the night the day,
Thou canst not then be false to any man.
Farewell. My blessing season this in thee.

LAERTES

Most humbly do I take my leave, Mother.
Farewell, Ophelia, and remember well
What I have said to you.

OPHELIA

'Tis in my memory locked,
And you yourself shall keep the key of it.

LAERTES

Farewell.

(exits)

POLONIUS

What is 't, Ophelia, he hath said to you?

OPHELIA

So please you, something touching the Lord
    Hamlet.
He hath, Mother, of late made many tenders
Of his affection to me.

POLONIUS

Do you believe his "tenders," as you call them?

OPHELIA

I do not know, Mother, what I should think.

POLONIUS

'Tis told me he hath very oft of late
Given private time to you, and you yourself
Have of your audience been most free and
    bounteous.
If it be so (as so 'tis put on me,
And that in way of caution), I must tell you
You do not understand yourself so clearly

          HAMLET, PRINCE OF DENMARK

As it behooves my daughter and your honor.

OPHELIA
    Mother! He hath importuned me with love
    In honorable fashion--

POLONIUS
    When the blood burns, how prodigal the soul
    Lends the tongue vows. From this time
    Be something scanter of your maiden presence.
    Set your entreatments at a higher rate
    Than a command to parle. For Lord Hamlet,
    Believe so much in him that he is young,
    And with a larger tether may he walk
    Than may be given you. In few, Ophelia,
    Do not believe his vows. This is for all:
    I would not, in plain terms, from this time forth
    Have you so slander any moment leisure
    As to give words or talk with the Lord Hamlet.

OPHELIA
    I shall obey.

SCENE FOUR
the battlements
midnight

HAMLET

>The air bites shrewdly; it is very cold.

HORATIO

>It is a nipping and an eager air.

HAMLET

>What hour now?

HORATIO

>I think it lacks of twelve.

HAMLET

>No, it is struck.

HORATIO

>Indeed, I heard it not. It then draws near the season
>Wherein the spirit held his wont to walk.
>Look, my lord, it comes.

>*The Ghost appears*

HAMLET

>Angels and ministers of grace, defend us!
>Be thou a spirit of health or goblin damned,
>Bring with thee airs from heaven or blasts from hell,
>Be thy intents wicked or charitable,
>Thou com'st in such a questionable shape
>That I will speak to thee. I'll call thee "Hamlet,"
>"King," "Father," "Royal Dane." O, answer me!

          HAMLET, PRINCE OF DENMARK

Let me not burst in ignorance, but tell
Why thy canonized bones, hearsed in death,
Have burst their cerements; why the sepulcher,
Wherein we saw thee quietly interred,
Hath oped his ponderous and marble jaws
To cast thee up again. What may this mean
That thou, dead corse, again in complete steel,
Revisits thus the glimpses of the moon,
Making night hideous, and we fools of nature
So horridly to shake our disposition
With thoughts beyond the reaches of our souls?
Say, why is this? Wherefore? What should we do?

HORATIO
It beckons you to go away with it
As if it some impartment did desire
To you alone.

HAMLET
                    Then I will follow it.

HORATIO
Do not, my lord.

HAMLET
                         Why, what should be the fear?
I do not set my life at a pin's fee.
And for my soul, what can it do to that,
Being a thing immortal as itself?

HORATIO
What if it tempt you toward the flood, my lord?
Or to the dreadful summit of the cliff,
And there assume some other horrible form
Which might deprive your sovereignty of reason

And draw you into madness? Think of it.
The very place puts toys of desperation,
Without more motive, into every brain
That looks so many fathoms to the sea
And hears it roar beneath.

HAMLET
                              My fate cries out.
I say, away! Go on. I'll follow thee.

Exit Hamlet and the Ghost

HORATIO
He waxes desperate with imagination.
Something is rotten in the state of Denmark.

<h1 style="text-align:center">SCENE FIVE</h1>
another section of the battlements

HAMLET
>Whither wilt thou lead me? Speak. I'll go no further.

GHOST
>Mark me.

HAMLET
>I will.

GHOST
>My hour is almost come
>When I to sulf'rous and tormenting flames
>Must render up myself.

HAMLET
>Alas, poor ghost!

GHOST
>Pity me not, but lend thy serious hearing
>To what I shall unfold.

HAMLET
>Speak. I am bound to hear.

GHOST
>So art thou to revenge, when thou shalt hear.

HAMLET
>What?

GHOST
>I am thy father's spirit,
>Doomed for a certain term to walk the night

And for the day confined to fast in fires
Till the foul crimes done in my days of nature
Are burnt and purged away. List, list, O list!
If thou didst ever thy dear father love--

HAMLET
O God!

GHOST
Revenge his foul and most unnatural murder.

HAMLET
Murder?

GHOST
Murder most foul, as in the best it is,
But this most foul, strange, and unnatural.

HAMLET
Haste me to know 't, that I, with wings as swift
As meditation or the thoughts of love,
May sweep to my revenge.

GHOST
Now, Hamlet, hear.
'Tis given out that, sleeping in my orchard,
A serpent stung me. But know, thou noble youth,
The serpent that did sting thy father's life
Now wears his crown.

HAMLET
O, my prophetic soul! My uncle!

GHOST
Ay, that incestuous, that adulterate beast.
But soft, methinks I scent the morning air.

Brief let me be. Sleeping within my orchard,
My custom always of the afternoon,
Thus was I, sleeping, by a brother's hand
Of life, of crown, of queen at once dispatched,
O horrible, O horrible, most horrible!
If thou hast nature in thee, bear it not.
Let not the royal bed of Denmark be
A couch for luxury and damned incest.
But, howsomever thou pursues this act,
Taint not thy mind, nor let thy soul contrive
Against thy mother aught. Leave her to heaven
And to those thorns that in her bosom lodge
To prick and sting her. Fare thee well at once.
Adieu, adieu, adieu. Remember me.
       (*vanishes*)

HAMLET
O all you host of heaven! O Earth! What else?
And shall I couple hell? O fie! Hold, hold, my heart,
And you, my sinews, grow not instant old,
But bear me stiffly up. Remember thee?
Yea, from the table of my memory
I'll wipe away all trivial, fond records,
All saws of books, all forms, all pressures past,
That youth and observation copied there,
And thy commandment all alone shall live
Within the book and volume of my brain.
O most pernicious woman!
O villain, villain, smiling, damned villain!
My tables--meet it is I set it down
That one may smile and smile and be a villain.
At least I am sure it may be so in Denmark.
It is "adieu, adieu, remember me."
I have sworn 't.

William Shakespeare

HORATIO

(*offstage*) My lord, my lord! Lord Hamlet.

HAMLET

So be it.

Enter Horatio

HORATIO

What news, my lord?

HAMLET

O, wonderful!

HORATIO

Good my lord, tell it.

HAMLET

No, you will reveal it.

HORATIO

Not I, my lord. By heaven, my lord not I.

HAMLET

How say you, then? Would heart of man once think
    it?
But you'll be secret?

HORATIO

Ay, by heaven, my lord.

HAMLET

There's never a villain dwelling in all Denmark
But he's an arrant knave.

                  HAMLET, PRINCE OF DENMARK

HORATIO

> There needs no ghost, my lord, come from the
>> grave
> To tell us this.

HAMLET

>> Why, right, you are in the right.
> And so, without more circumstance at all,
> I hold it fit that we shake hands and part,
> You, as your business and desire shall point you
> (For every man hath business and desire,
> Such as it is), and for my own poor part,
> I will go pray.

HORATIO

> These are but wild and whirling words, my lord.

HAMLET

> I am sorry they offend you, heartily;
> Yes, faith, heartily.

HORATIO

>> There's no offense, my lord.

HAMLET

> Yes, by Saint Patrick, but there is, Horatio.
> It is an honest ghost, that let me tell you.
> For your desire to know what is between us,
> O'ermaster 't as you may. And now, good friend,
> Give me one poor request.

HORATIO

>> What is 't, my lord?

HAMLET

> Never make known what you have seen tonight.

HORATIO
    My lord, I will not.

HAMLET
    Nay, but swear 't.

HORATIO
                    I have sworn, my lord, already.

GHOST
    (*offstage*) Swear.

HORATIO
    Propose the oath, my lord.

HAMLET
    Never to speak of this that you have seen.

GHOST
    (*offstage*) Swear.

HORATIO
    O day and night, but this is wondrous strange.

HAMLET
    There are more things in heaven and earth, Horatio,
    Than are dreamt of in your philosophy. But come.
    Here, as before, never, so help you mercy,
    How strange or odd some'er I bear myself
    (As I perchance hereafter shall think meet
    To put an antic disposition on)
    That you, at such times seeing me, never shall,
    With arms encumbered thus, or this headshake,
    Or by pronouncing of some doubtful phrase,
    Or such ambiguous giving-out, to note
    That you know aught of me - this do swear.

                    HAMLET, PRINCE OF DENMARK

GHOST

> (*offstage*) Swear.

HAMLET

> Rest, rest, perturbed spirit. - So, gentle friend,
> With all my love I do commend me to you,
> And what so poor a man as Hamlet is
> May do t' express his love and friending to you,
> God willing, shall not lack. Let us go in together.
> And still your finger on your lips, I pray.
> The time is out of joint. O cursed spite
> That ever I was born to set it right!

SCENE SIX

Polonius' house

POLONIUS

    How now, Ophelia, what's the matter?

OPHELIA

    O, Mother! Mother, I have been so affrighted!

POLONIUS

    With what, i' th' name of God?

OPHELIA

    Mother, as I was sewing in my closet,
    Lord Hamlet, with his doublet all unbraced,
    Pale as his shirt, his knees knocking each other,
    And with a look so piteous in purport
    As if he had been loosed out of hell
    To speak of horrors - he comes before me.

POLONIUS

    Mad for thy love?

OPHELIA

               My lord, I do not know,
    But truly I do fear it.

POLONIUS

                 What said he?

OPHELIA

    He took me by the wrist and held me hard.
    And, with his other hand thus o'er his brow,
    He falls to such perusal of my face
    As he would draw it. Long stayed he so.

At last, a little shaking of mine arm,
And thrice his head thus waving up and down,
He raised a sigh so piteous and profound
As it did seem to shatter all his bulk
And end his being. That done, he lets me go,
And, with his head over his shoulder turned,
He seemed to find his way without his eyes,
For out o' doors he went without their helps
And to the last bended their light on me.

POLONIUS
    This is the very ecstasy of love.
    What, have you given him any hard words of late?

OPHELIA
    No, good Mother, but as you did command
    I did repel his letters and denied
    His access to me.

POLONIUS
                  That hath made him mad.
    I am sorry that with better heed and judgment
    I had not coted him. I feared he did but trifle
    And meant to wrack thee. Go we to the King.
    This must be known, which, being kept close, might
        move
    More grief to hide than hate to utter love.
    Come.

SCENE SEVEN
the throne room

Rosencrantz and Guildenstern alone.
Enter Claudius and Gertrude.

CLAUDIUS

    Welcome, dear Rosencrantz and Guildenstern.
    The need we have to use you did provoke
    Our hasty sending. Something have you heard
    Of Hamlet's transformation, so call it,
    Sith nor th' exterior nor the inward man
    Resembles that it was. What it should be,
    More than his father's death, that thus hath put him
    So much from th' understanding of himself
    I cannot dream.

GERTRUDE

              He hath much talked of you,
    And sure I am two men there is not living
    To whom he more adheres. If it will please you
    As to expend your time with us awhile,
    Your visitation shall receive such thanks
    As fits a king's remembrance.

Exit Gertrude, Rosencrantz, and
Guildenstern. Enter Polonius.

POLONIUS

    Th' ambassadors from Norway, my good lord,
    Are joyfully returned.

CLAUDIUS
>Thou still hast been the mother of good news.

POLONIUS
>Have I, my lord? I assure my good liege
>I hold my duty as I hold my soul,
>And I do think, or else this brain of mine
>Hunts not the trail of policy so sure
>As it hath used to do, that I have found
>The very cause of Hamlet's lunacy.

CLAUDIUS
>O, speak of that! That do I long to hear.
>>(*enter Gertrude*)
>She tells me, my dear Gertrude, she hath found
>The head and source of all your son's distemper.

GERTRUDE
>I doubt it is no other but the main -
>His father's death and our o'erhasty marriage.

CLAUDIUS
>Well, we shall sift him.

POLONIUS
>I will be brief. Your noble son is mad.
>"Mad" call I it, for, to define true madness,
>What is 't but to be nothing else but mad?
>But let that go.

GERTRUDE
>>More matter with less art.

POLONIUS
>Madam, I swear I use no art at all.
>That he's mad, 'tis true; 'tis true 'tis pity,

William Shakespeare   29

And pity 'tis 'tis true--a foolish figure,
But farewell it, for I will use no art.
I have a daughter (have while she is mine)
Who, in her duty and obedience, mark,
Hath given me this. Now gather and surmise.
             (reads)
"To the celestial, and my soul's idol, the most
beautified Ophelia - In her excellent white bosom,
these, etc. -"

GERTRUDE
        Came this from Hamlet to her?

POLONIUS
        Good madam, stay awhile. I will be faithful.
             (reads)
        "Doubt thou the stars are fire,
           Doubt that the sun doth move,
        Doubt truth to be a liar,
           But never doubt I love.

        O dear Ophelia, I am ill at these numbers. I have
        not art to reckon my groans, but that I love thee
        best, O most best, believe it. Adieu.

               Thine evermore, most dear lady, whilst
               this machine is to him,
                          Hamlet"

CLAUDIUS
        Do you think 'tis this?

GERTRUDE
        It may be, very like.

POLONIUS

> Take this from this, if this be otherwise.
> If circumstances lead me, I will find
> Where truth is hid, though it were hid, indeed,
> Within the center.

CLAUDIUS

> How may we try it further?

POLONIUS

> You know sometimes he walks four hours together
> Here in the lobby.

GERTRUDE

> So he does indeed.

POLONIUS

> At such a time I'll loose my daughter to him.
> Be you and I behind an arras then.
> Mark the encounter. If he love her not,
> And be not from his reason fall'n thereon,
> Let me be no assistant for a state,
> But keep a farm and carters.

CLAUDIUS

> We will try it.

GERTRUDE

> But look where sadly the poor wretch comes
> reading.

POLONIUS

> Away, I do beseech you both, away.
> I'll board him presently.
> *(exit Claudius and Gertrude as Hamlet
> enters, reading)*

POLONIUS

                                    O, give me leave.
How does my good Lord Hamlet?

HAMLET

Well, God-a-mercy.

POLONIUS

Do you know me, my lord?

HAMLET

Excellent well. You are a fishmonger.

POLONIUS

Not I, my lord.

HAMLET

Then I would you were so honest a man.

POLONIUS

Honest, my lord?

HAMLET

Ay. To be honest, as this world goes, is to be one
man picked out of ten thousand.

POLONIUS

That's very true, my lord.

HAMLET

Have you a daughter?

POLONIUS

I have, my lord.

HAMLET

Let her not walk i' th' sun. Conception is a blessing, but, as your daughter may conceive, friend, look to 't.

POLONIUS

(*aside*) Still harping on my daughter. Yet he knew me not at first; he said I was a fishmonger. And truly, in my youth, I suffered much extremity for love, very near this. (*to Hamlet*) What do you read, my lord?

HAMLET

Words, words, words.

POLONIUS

What is the matter, my lord?

HAMLET

Between who?

POLONIUS

I mean the matter that you read, my lord.

HAMLET

Slanders; for the satirical rogue says here that old men have gray beards, that their faces are wrinkled, and that they have a plentiful lack of wit. All which, though I most powerfully and potently believe, yet I hold it not honesty to have it thus set down; for yourself, shall grow old as I am, if, like a crab, you could go backward.

POLONIUS

Though this be madness, yet there is method in 't. Will you walk out of the air, my lord?

HAMLET

Into my grave?

POLONIUS

Indeed, that's out of the air. How pregnant sometimes his replies are! My lord, I will take my leave of you.

HAMLET

You cannot take from me anything that I will more willingly part withal - except my life, except my life, except my life.

POLONIUS

Fare you well, my lord.
(exits)

HAMLET

These tedious old fools.

Rosencrantz and Guildenstern enter

HAMLET

My excellent good friends! How dost thou, Guildenstern? Ah, Rosencrantz! How do you both?

ROSENCRANTZ

As the indifferent children of the earth.

GUILDENSTERN

Happy in that we are not overhappy.

HAMLET

Nor the soles of her shoe?

                    HAMLET, PRINCE OF DENMARK

ROSENCRANTZ

Neither, my lord.

HAMLET

Then you live about her waist, or in the middle of
her favors?

GUILDENSTERN

Faith, her privates we.

HAMLET

What news?

ROSENCRANTZ

None, my lord, but that the world's grown honest.

HAMLET

Then is doomsday near. But your news is not true.
What have you, my good friends, deserved at the
hands of Fortune that she sends you to prison
hither?

GUILDENSTERN

Prison, my lord?

HAMLET

Denmark's a prison.

ROSENCRANTZ

Then is the world one.

HAMLET

A goodly one, in which there are many confines,
wards, and dungeons, Denmark being one o' th'
worst.

ROSENCRANTZ

> We think not so, my lord.

HAMLET

> Why, then, 'tis none to you, for there is nothing
> either good or bad but thinking makes it so. To me,
> it is a prison.

ROSENCRANTZ

> Why, then, your ambition makes it one. 'Tis too
> narrow for your mind.

HAMLET

> O God, I could be bounded in a nutshell and count
> myself a king of infinite space, were it not that I
> have bad dreams.

GUILDENSTERN

> Which dreams, indeed, are ambition, for the very
> substance of the ambitious is merely the shadow of
> a dream.

HAMLET

> A dream itself is but a shadow.

ROSENCRANTZ

> Truly, and I hold ambition of so airy and light a
> quality that it is but a shadow's shadow.

HAMLET

> Then are our beggars bodies, and our monarchs
> and outstretched heroes the beggars' shadows.
> What make you at Elsinore?

ROSENCRANTZ

> To visit you, my lord, no other occasion.

　　　　HAMLET, PRINCE OF DENMARK

HAMLET

Beggar that I am, I am even poor in thanks; but I thank you, and sure, dear friends, my thanks are too dear a halfpenny. You were sent for, and there is a kind of confession in your looks which your modesties have not craft enough to color. I know the good King and Queen have sent for you.

ROSENCRANTZ

To what end, my lord?

HAMLET

I will tell you why; so shall my anticipation prevent your discovery, and your secrecy to the King and Queen molt no feather. I have of late, but wherefore I know not, lost all my mirth, forgone all custom of exercises, and, indeed, it goes so heavily with my disposition that this goodly frame, the Earth, seems to me a sterile promontory; this most excellent canopy, the air, look you, this brave o'erhanging firmament, this majestical roof, fretted with golden fire - why, it appeareth nothing to me but a foul and pestilent congregation of vapors. What a piece of work is a man, how noble in reason, how infinite in faculties, in form and moving how express and admirable; in action how like an angel, in apprehension how like a god: the beauty of the world, the paragon of animals - and yet, to me, what is this quintessence of dust? Man delights not me, no, nor women neither, though by your smiling you seem to say so.

GUILDENSTERN

My lord, there was no such stuff in my thoughts.

HAMLET

> Why did you laugh, then, when I said "man delights
> not me"?

ROSENCRANTZ

> To think, my lord, if you delight not in man, what
> Lenten entertainment the players shall receive from
> you.

HAMLET

> He that plays the king shall be welcome. What
> players are they?

ROSENCRANTZ

> The best actors in the world, either for tragedy,
> comedy, history, pastoral, pastoral-comical,
> historical-pastoral, tragical-historical, tragical-
> comical-historical-pastoral, scene individable, or
> poem unlimited. Seneca cannot be too heavy, nor
> Plautus too light. For the law of writ and the liberty,
> we are the only men.

HAMLET

> You are welcome. We'll have a speech straight.
> Come, give us a taste of your quality. Come, a
> passionate speech.

ROSENCRANTZ

> What speech, my good lord?

HAMLET

> I heard thee speak me a speech once, but it was
> never acted, or, if it was, not above once. But it was
> (as I received it) an excellent play, well digested in
> the scenes, set down with as much modesty as

     HAMLET, PRINCE OF DENMARK

cunning. One speech in 't I chiefly loved. 'Twas
Aeneas' tale to Dido, and thereabout of it
especially when he speaks of Priam's slaughter. If it
live in your memory, begin at this line - let me see,
let me see:

"With eyes like carbuncles, the hellish Pyrrhus
Old grandsire Priam seeks."

So, proceed you.

ROSENCRANTZ
                              "Anon he finds him
Striking too short at Greeks. Unequal matched,
Pyrrhus at Priam drives, in rage strikes wide;
But with the whiff and wind of his fell sword
Th' unnerved father falls. Then senseless Ilium,
Seeming to feel this blow, with flaming top
Stoops to his base, and with a hideous crash
Takes prisoner Pyrrhus' ear. For lo, his sword,
Which was declining on the milky head
Of reverend Priam, seemed i' th' air to stick.
So as a painted tyrant Pyrrhus stood
And, like a neutral to his will and matter,
Did nothing.
But as we often see against some storm
A silence in the heavens, the rack stand still,
The bold winds speechless, and the orb below
As hush as death, anon the dreadful thunder
Doth rend the region; so, after Pyrrhus' pause,
Aroused vengeance sets him new a-work,
And never did the Cyclops' hammers fall
On Mars's armor, forged for proof eterne,
With less remorse than Pyrrhus' bleeding sword

Now falls on Priam.
Out, out, thou strumpet Fortune! All you gods
In general synod take away her power,
Break all the spokes and fellies from her wheel,
And bowl the round nave down the hill of heaven
As low as to the fiends!"

GUILDENSTERN
This is too long.

HAMLET
Prithee say on. Say on; come to Hecuba.

ROSENCRANTZ
"But who, ah woe, had seen the moblèd queen -"

HAMLET
The moblèd queen.

GUILDENSTERN
That's good. "Moblèd queen" is good.

ROSENCRANTZ
"Run barefoot up and down, threat'ning the flames.
Who this had seen, with tongue in venom steeped,
'Gainst Fortune's state would treason have
    pronounced.
But if the gods themselves did see her then
When she saw Pyrrhus make malicious sport
In mincing with his sword her husband's limbs,
The instant burst of clamor that she made
(Unless things mortal move them not at all)
Would have made milch the burning eyes of
    heaven
And passion in the gods."

HAMLET

Prithee, no more. Can you play "The Murder of
Gonzago"?

ROSENCRANTZ

Ay, my lord.

HAMLET

We'll ha 't tomorrow night. You could, for a need,
study a speech of some dozen or sixteen lines,
which I would set down and insert in 't, could you
not?

ROSENCRANTZ

Ay, my lord.

HAMLET

Very well. I'll leave you till night. You are welcome
to Elsinore. But my uncle-father and aunt-mother
are deceived.

GUILDENSTERN

In what, my dear lord?

HAMLET

I am but mad north-north-west: when the wind is
southerly I know a hawk from a handsaw.

ROSENCRANTZ

Good my lord.

HAMLET

Ay, so, good-bye to you.
                (exit Rosencrantz and Guildenstern)
                                Now I am alone.
O, what a rogue and peasant slave am I!

Is it not monstrous that this player here,
But in a fiction, in a dream of passion,
Could force her soul so to her own conceit
That from her working all her visage wanned,
Tears in her eyes, distraction in her aspect,
A broken voice, and her whole function suiting
With forms to her conceit - and all for nothing!
For Hecuba!
What's Hecuba to her, or she to Hecuba,
That she should weep for her? What would she do
Had she the motive and the cue for passion
That I have? She would drown the stage with tears
And cleave the general ear with horrid speech,
Make mad the guilty and appall the free,
Confound the ignorant and amaze indeed
The very faculties of eyes and ears.
Yet I,
A dull and muddy-mettled rascal, peak
Like John-a-dreams, unpregnant of my cause,
And can say nothing - no, not for a king
Upon whose property and most dear life
A damned defeat was made. Am I a coward?
Who calls me "villain"? Who does me this?
Ha! 'Swounds, I should take it! For it cannot be
But I am pigeon-livered and lack gall
To make oppression bitter, or ere this
I should have fatted all the region kites
With this slave's offal. Bloody, bawdy villain!
Remorseless, treacherous, lecherous, kindless
    villain!
About, my brains! - Hum, I have heard
That guilty creatures sitting at a play
Have, by the very cunning of the scene,
Been struck so to the soul that presently
They have proclaimed their malefactions;

                     HAMLET, PRINCE OF DENMARK

For murder, though it have no tongue, will speak
With most miraculous organ. I'll have these players
Play something like the murder of my father
Before mine uncle. I'll observe his looks;
I'll tent him to the quick. If he do blench,
I know my course. The spirit that I have seen
May be a devil, and the devil hath power
T' assume a pleasing shape; yea, and perhaps,
Out of my weakness and my melancholy,
Abuses me to damn me. I'll have grounds
More relative than this. The play's the thing
Wherein I'll catch the conscience of the King.

William Shakespeare

<h1 style="text-align:center">SCENE EIGHT</h1>
the courtyard

POLONIUS

    Ophelia, walk you here. - Gracious, so please you,
    We will bestow ourselves. - Read on this book.
    I hear him coming. Let's withdraw, my lord.

        Claudius and Polonius conceal
        themselves. Enter Hamlet.

HAMLET

    The fair Ophelia. - Nymph, in thy orisons
    Be all my sins remembered.

OPHELIA

                    Good my lord,
    How does your Honor for this many a day?

HAMLET

    I humbly thank you, well.

OPHELIA

    My lord, I have remembrances of yours
    That I have longed long to redeliver.
    I pray you now receive them.

HAMLET

    No, not I. I never gave you aught.

OPHELIA

    My honored lord, you know right well you did,
    And with them words of so sweet breath composed
    As made the things more rich. Their perfume lost,

Take these again, for to the noble mind
Rich gifts wax poor when givers prove unkind.
There, my lord.

HAMLET

Ha, ha! Are you honest?

OPHELIA

My lord?

HAMLET

Are you fair?

OPHELIA

What means your Lordship?

HAMLET

That if you be honest and fair, your honesty should
admit no discourse to your beauty.

OPHELIA

Could beauty, my lord, have better commerce than
with honesty?

HAMLET

Ay, truly, for the power of beauty will sooner
transform honesty from what it is to a bawd than
the force of honesty can translate beauty into his
likeness. This was sometime a paradox, but now the
time gives it proof. I did love you once.

OPHELIA

Indeed, my lord, you made me believe so.

HAMLET

You should not have believed me, for virtue cannot
so inoculate our old stock but we shall relish of it. I
loved you not.

OPHELIA

I was the more deceived.

HAMLET

Get thee to a nunnery. Why wouldst thou be a
breeder of sinners? I am myself indifferent honest,
but yet I could accuse me of such things that it
were better my mother had not borne me: I am
very proud, revengeful, ambitious, with more
offenses at my beck than I have thoughts to put
them in, imagination to give them shape, or time to
act them in. What should such fellows as I do
crawling between earth and heaven? We are arrant
knaves all; believe none of us. Go thy ways to a
nunnery. Where's your mother?

OPHELIA

At home, my lord.

HAMLET

Let the doors be shut upon her that she may play
the fool nowhere but in her own house. Farewell. If
thou dost marry, I'll give thee this plague for thy
dowry: be thou as chaste as ice, as pure as snow,
thou shalt not escape calumny. Get thee to a
nunnery, farewell. Or if thou wilt needs marry, marry
a fool, for wise men know well enough what
monsters you make of them. To a nunnery, go, and
quickly too. Farewell.

OPHELIA

Heavenly powers, restore him!

HAMLET

I have heard of your paintings too. God hath given
you one face, and you make yourselves another.
You jig and amble, and you lisp; you nickname
God's creatures and make your wantonness your
ignorance. Go to, I'll no more on 't. It hath made
me mad. I say we will have no more marriage.
Those that are married already, all but one, shall
live. The rest shall keep as they are. To a nunnery,
go.

(*exits*)

OPHELIA

O, what a noble mind is here o'erthrown!
The courtier's, soldier's, scholar's, eye, tongue,
    sword,
Th' expectancy and rose of the fair state,
The glass of fashion and the mold of form,
Th' observed of all observers, quite, quite down!
And I, of ladies most deject and wretched,
That sucked the honey of his musicked vows,
Now see that noble and most sovereign reason,
Like sweet bells jangled, out of time and harsh;
That unmatched form and stature of blown youth
Blasted with ecstasy. O, woe is me
T' have seen what I have seen, see what I see!

Enter Claudius and Polonius

CLAUDIUS

Love? His affections do not that way tend;
Nor what he spake, though it lacked form a little,
Was not like madness. There's something in his soul
O'er which his melancholy sits on brood,
And I do doubt the hatch and the disclose
Will be some danger; which for to prevent,
I have in quick determination
Thus set it down: he shall with speed to England.

POLONIUS

It shall do well. But yet do I believe
The origin and commencement of his grief
Sprung from neglected love. - How now, Ophelia?
You need not tell us what Lord Hamlet said;
We heard it all. -
            (exit Ophelia)
                    My lord, do as you please,
But, if you hold it fit, after the play
Let his queen-mother all alone entreat him
To show his grief. But if she find him not,
To England send him, or confine him where
Your wisdom best shall think.

CLAUDIUS

                            It shall be so.
Madness in great ones must not unwatched go.

SCENE NINE
the theater

Hamlet, Rosencrantz, and Guildenstern
prepare the stage.

HAMLET
> Speak the speech, I pray you, as I pronounced it to
> you, trippingly on the tongue. Nor do not saw the
> air too much with your hand, thus, but use all
> gently. Suit the action to the word, the word to the
> action, with this special observance, that you
> o'erstep not the modesty of nature.

ROSENCRANTZ
> I hope we have reformed that indifferently with us,
> sir.

HAMLET
> O, reform it altogether. And let those that play your
> clowns speak no more than is set down for them.
> Go make you ready.

> *Exit Rosencrantz and Guildenstern. Enter*
> *Horatio.*

HAMLET
> What ho, Horatio!
> There is a play tonight before the King.
> One scene of it comes near the circumstance
> Which I have told thee of my father's death.
> I prithee, when thou seest that act afoot,
> Observe my uncle. Give him heedful note,

For I mine eyes will rivet to his face,
And, after, we will both our judgments join
In censure of his seeming.

HORATIO
                              Well, my lord.
If he steal aught the whilst this play is playing
And 'scape detecting, I will pay the theft.

HAMLET
They are coming to the play. I must be idle. Get
you a place.

*Enter Claudius, Gertrude, Polonius, and
Ophelia.*

CLAUDIUS
How fares our cousin Hamlet?

HAMLET
Excellent, i' faith. (*to Polonius*) You played once i'
th' university, you say?

POLONIUS
That did I, my lord, and was accounted a good
actor.

HAMLET
What did you enact?

POLONIUS
I did enact Julius Caesar. I was killed i' th' Capitol.
Brutus killed me.

                    HAMLET, PRINCE OF DENMARK

HAMLET

It was a brute part of him to kill so capital a calf
there. Be the players ready?

POLONIUS

Ay, my lord. They stay upon your patience.

GERTRUDE

Come hither, my dear Hamlet, sit by me.

HAMLET

No, good mother. Here's metal more attractive.

POLONIUS

(*to Claudius*) Oh, ho! Do you mark that?

HAMLET

Lady, shall I lie in your lap?

OPHELIA

No, my lord.

HAMLET

I mean, my head upon your lap?

OPHELIA

Ay, my lord.

HAMLET

Do you think I meant country matters?

OPHELIA

I think nothing, my lord.

HAMLET

That's a fair thought to lie between maids' legs.

OPHELIA

What is, my lord?

HAMLET

Nothing.

OPHELIA

You are merry, my lord.

HAMLET

Who, I?

OPHELIA

Ay, my lord.

HAMLET

What should a man do but be merry? For look you
how cheerfully my mother looks, and my father
died within 's two hours.

OPHELIA

Nay, 'tis twice two months, my lord.

HAMLET

So long? Nay, then, let the devil wear black, for I'll
have a suit of sables. O heavens, die two months
ago, and not forgotten yet? Then there's hope a
great man's memory may outlive his life half a year

OPHELIA

You are naught, you are naught. I'll mark the play.

*The lights go down as Guildenstern
enters*

          HAMLET, PRINCE OF DENMARK

GUILDENSTERN (AS PROLOGUE)
    For us and for our tragedy,
    Here stooping to your clemency,
    We beg your hearing patiently.
            (exits)

HAMLET
    Is this a prologue or the posy of a ring?

OPHELIA
    'Tis brief, my lord.

HAMLET
    As woman's love.

                    Enter the Rosencrantz as the Player
                    Queen and Guildenstern as the Player
                    King.

GUILDENSTERN (AS THE PLAYER KING)
    Full thirty times hath Phoebus' cart gone round
    Neptune's salt wash and Tellus' orbed ground,
    Since love our hearts and Hymen did our hands
    Unite commutual in most sacred bands.

ROSENCRANTZ (AS THE PLAYER QUEEN)
    So many journeys may the sun and moon
    Make us again count o'er ere love be done!
    Now what my love is, proof hath made you know,
    And, as my love is sized, my fear is so:
    Where love is great, the littlest doubts are fear;
    Where little fears grow great, great love grows
        there.

GUILDENSTERN (AS THE PLAYER KING)
    Faith, I must leave thee, love, and shortly too.
    My operant powers their functions leave to do.
    And thou shall live in this fair world behind,
    Honored, beloved; and haply one as kind
    For husband shalt thou-

ROSENCRANTZ (AS THE PLAYER QUEEN)
                            O, confound the rest!
    Such love must needs be treason in my breast.
    In second husband let me be accurst.
    None wed the second but who killed the first.
    The instances that second marriage move
    Are base respects of thrift, but none of love.
    A second time I kill my husband dead
    When second husband kisses me in bed.

GUILDENSTERN (AS THE PLAYER KING)
    I do believe you think what now you speak,
    But what we do determine oft we break.

ROSENCRANTZ (AS THE PLAYER QUEEN)
    Both here and hence pursue me lasting strife,
    If, once a widow, ever I be wife.

HAMLET
    If she should break it now!

GUILDENSTERN (AS THE PLAYER KING)
    'Tis deeply sworn. Sweet, leave me here awhile.
    My spirits grow dull, and fain I would beguile
    The tedious day with sleep.

ROSENCRANTZ (AS THE PLAYER QUEEN)
>   Sleep rock thy brain,
> And never come mischance between us twain.

The Player King sleeps. Exit the Player Queen as the lights rise for "intermission."

HAMLET

Madam, how like you this play?

GERTRUDE

The lady doth protest too much, methinks.

HAMLET

O, but she'll keep her word.

CLAUDIUS

Have you heard the argument? Is there no offense in 't?

HAMLET

No, no, they do but jest, poison in jest. No offense i' th' world.

CLAUDIUS

What do you call the play?

HAMLET

"The Mousetrap." This play is the image of a murder done in Vienna. 'Tis a knavish piece of work, but what of that? Your Majesty and we that have free souls, it touches us not.

HAMLET
This is one Lucianus, nephew to the king.

OPHELIA
You are as good as a chorus, my lord.

HAMLET
I could interpret between you and your love.

OPHELIA
You are keen, my lord, you are keen.

HAMLET
It would cost you a groaning to take off mine edge.

OPHELIA
Still better and worse.

HAMLET
He poisons him i' th' garden for his estate. You shall
see anon how the murderer gets the love of
Gonzago's wife.

ROSENCRANTZ (AS LUCIANUS)
Thoughts black, hands apt, drugs fit, and time
    agreeing,
Confederate season, else no creature seeing,
Thou mixture rank, of midnight weeds collected,
With Hecate's ban thrice blasted, thrice infected,
Thy natural magic and dire property
On wholesome life usurp immediately.

OPHELIA
The King rises!

HAMLET
What, frighted with false fire?

GERTRUDE
How fares my lord?

POLONIUS
Give o'er the play.

CLAUDIUS
Give me some light. Away!

POLONIUS
Lights, lights, lights!

Exeunt all but Hamlet and Horatio

HAMLET
O good Horatio, I'll take the ghost's word for a
thousand pound. Didst perceive?

HORATIO
Very well, my lord.

HAMLET
Upon the talk of the poisoning?

HORATIO
I did very well note him.

*Exit Horatio. Enter Rosencrantz and
Guildenstern*

GUILDENSTERN
Good my lord, vouchsafe me a word with you.

HAMLET
Sir, a whole history.

GUILDENSTERN
The King, sir -

HAMLET
Ay, sir, what of him?

GUILDENSTERN
Is in his retirement marvelous distempered.

HAMLET
With drink, sir?

GUILDENSTERN
No, my lord, with choler. Good my lord, put your
discourse into some frame and start not so wildly
from my affair.

HAMLET
I am tame, sir. Pronounce.

       HAMLET, PRINCE OF DENMARK

GUILDENSTERN

The Queen your mother, in most great affliction of
spirit, hath sent me to you.

HAMLET

You are welcome.

GUILDENSTERN

Nay, good my lord, this courtesy is not of the right
breed. If it shall please you to make me a
wholesome answer, I will do your mother's
commandment. If not, your pardon and my return
shall be the end of my business.

HAMLET

Sir, I cannot.

ROSENCRANTZ

What, my lord?

HAMLET

Make you a wholesome answer. My wit's diseased.
But, such answer as I can make, you shall command
- or, rather, as you say, my mother.

ROSENCRANTZ

She desires to speak with you in her closet ere you
go to bed.

HAMLET

We shall obey, were she ten times our mother.

ROSENCRANTZ

Good my lord, what is your cause of distemper?
You do surely bar the door upon your own liberty if
you deny your griefs to your friend.

HAMLET
    I lack advancement.

ROSENCRANTZ
    How can that be, when you have the voice of the
    King himself for your succession in Denmark?

HAMLET
    Ay, but "While the grass grows..."
    Why do you go about to recover the wind of me, as
    if you would drive me into a toil?

GUILDENSTERN
    O, my lord, if my duty be too bold, my love is too
    unmannerly.

HAMLET
    I do not well understand that. (*picking up a
    discarded recorder*) Will you play upon this pipe?

GUILDENSTERN
    My lord, I cannot.

HAMLET
    I pray you.

GUILDENSTERN
    Believe me, I cannot.

HAMLET
    I do beseech you.

GUILDENSTERN
    I know no touch of it, my lord.

HAMLET

It is as easy as lying. Look you, these are the stops.

GUILDENSTERN

But these cannot I command to any utt'rance of
harmony. I have not the skill.

HAMLET

Why, look you now, how unworthy a thing you
make of me! You would play upon me, you would
seem to know my stops, you would pluck out the
heart of my mystery, you would sound me from my
lowest note to the top of my compass; and there is
much music, excellent voice, in this little organ, yet
cannot you make it speak. Do you think I am easier
to be played on than a pipe? Call me what
instrument you will, though you can fret me, you
cannot play upon me.

Enter Polonius

POLONIUS

My lord, the Queen would speak with you, and
presently.

HAMLET

Then I will come to my mother by and by.

POLONIUS

I will say so.

HAMLET

"By and by" is easily said. Leave me, friends.

'Tis now the very witching time of night,
When churchyards yawn and hell itself breathes out
Contagion to this world. Now could I drink hot
    blood
And do such bitter business as the day
Would quake to look on. Soft, now to my mother.
Let me be cruel, not unnatural.
I will speak daggers to her, but use none.
My tongue and soul in this be hypocrites:
How in my words somever she be shent,
To give them seals never, my soul, consent.

SCENE TEN
the chapel

CLAUDIUS

O, my offense is rank, it smells to heaven;
It hath the primal eldest curse upon 't,
A brother's murder. Pray can I not,
Though inclination be as sharp as will.
My stronger guilt defeats my strong intent,
And, like a man to double business bound,
I stand in pause where I shall first begin
And both neglect. What if this cursed hand
Were thicker than itself with brother's blood?
Is there not rain enough in the sweet heavens
To wash it white as snow? Whereto serves mercy
But to confront the visage of offense?
And what's in prayer but this twofold force,
To be forestalled ere we come to fall,
Or pardoned being down? Then I'll look up.
My fault is past. But, O, what form of prayer
Can serve my turn? "Forgive me my foul murder"?
That cannot be, since I am still possessed
Of those effects for which I did the murder:
My crown, mine own ambition, and my queen.
May one be pardoned and retain th' offense?
In the corrupted currents of this world,
Offense's gilded hand may shove by justice,
And oft 'tis seen the wicked prize itself
Buys out the law. But 'tis not so above:
There is no shuffling; there the action lies
In his true nature, and we ourselves compelled,
Even to the teeth and forehead of our faults,
To give in evidence. What then? What rests?
Try what repentance can. What can it not?
Yet what can it, when one cannot repent?

William Shakespeare   63

Bow, stubborn knees, and heart with strings of steel
Be soft as sinews of the newborn babe.
All may be well.

Claudius kneels to pray. Enter Hamlet.

HAMLET
        Now might I do it pat, now he is a-praying,
        And now I'll do 't. And so he goes to heaven,
        And so am I revenged. That would be scanned:
        A villain kills my father, and for that,
        I, his sole son, do this same villain send
        To heaven.
        He took my father grossly, full of bread,
        With all his crimes broad blown, as flush as May;
        And how his audit stands who knows save heaven.
        But in our circumstance and course of thought
        'Tis heavy with him. And am I then revenged
        To take him in the purging of his soul,
        When he is fit and seasoned for his passage?
        No.
        When he is drunk asleep, or in his rage,
        Or in th' incestuous pleasure of his bed,
        At game, a-swearing, or about some act
        That has no relish of salvation in 't--
        Then trip him, that his heels may kick at heaven,
        And that his soul may be as damned and black
        As hell, whereto it goes. My mother stays.
        This physic but prolongs thy sickly days.
                (*exits*)

CLAUDIUS
    My words fly up, my thoughts remain below;
    Words without thoughts never to heaven go.

William Shakespeare

SCENE ELEVEN
Gertrude's chambers

POLONIUS
> He will come straight. I'll silence me even here.
> Pray you, be round with him.

HAMLET
> (*offstage*) Mother, mother, mother!

GERTRUDE
> I'll warrant you. Fear me not. Withdraw, I hear him
> coming.

> *Polonius hides behind a curtain. Enter
> Hamlet.*

HAMLET
> Now, mother, what's the matter?

GERTRUDE
> Hamlet, thou hast thy father much offended.

HAMLET
> Mother, you have my father much offended.

GERTRUDE
> Come, come, you answer with an idle tongue.

HAMLET
> Go, go, you question with a wicked tongue.

GERTRUDE
> Why, how now, Hamlet?

                    HAMLET, PRINCE OF DENMARK

HAMLET

What's the matter now?

GERTRUDE

Have you forgot me?

HAMLET

No, by the rood, not so.
You are the Queen, your husband's brother's wife,
And (would it were not so) you are my mother.

GERTRUDE

Nay, then I'll set those to you that can speak.

HAMLET

Come, come, and sit you down; you shall not
    budge.
You go not till I set you up a glass
Where you may see the inmost part of you.

GERTRUDE

What wilt thou do? Thou wilt not murder me?
Help, ho!

POLONIUS

(*hidden*) What ho! Help!

HAMLET

How now, a rat? Dead for a ducat, dead.

*Hamlet stabs Polonius through the
curtain.*

POLONIUS
   O, I am slain!

GERTRUDE
                    O me, what hast thou done?

HAMLET
   Nay, I know not. Is it the King?

GERTRUDE
   O, what a rash and bloody deed is this!

HAMLET
   A bloody deed. Almost as bad, good mother,
   As kill a king and marry with his brother.

GERTRUDE
   As kill a king?

HAMLET
                    Ay, lady, it was my word.
                    (reveals Polonius' body)
   Thou wretched, rash, intruding fool, farewell.
   I took thee for thy better. Take thy fortune.
   Thou find'st to be too busy is some danger.
   Leave wringing of your hands. Peace, sit you down,
   And let me wring your heart; for so I shall
   If damned custom have not brazed it so
   That it be proof and bulwark against sense.

GERTRUDE
   What have I done, that thou dar'st wag thy tongue
   In noise so rude against me?

HAMLET

                                Such an act
        That blurs the grace and blush of modesty,
        Calls virtue hypocrite, makes marriage vows
        As false as dicers' oaths.

GERTRUDE

                            Ay me, what act
        That roars so loud and thunders in the index?

HAMLET
        Look here upon this picture and on this,
        The counterfeit presentment of two brothers.
        This was your husband. Look you now what follows.
        Here is your husband, like a mildewed ear
        Blasting his wholesome brother. Have you eyes?
        You cannot call it love, for at your age
        The heyday in the blood is tame, it's humble
        And waits upon the judgment; and what judgment
        Would step from this to this? Where is thy blush?
        Rebellious hell!

GERTRUDE
        O Hamlet, speak no more!
        Thou turn'st my eyes into my very soul,
        And there I see such black and grained spots
        As will not leave their tinct.

HAMLET

                            Nay, but to live
        In the rank sweat of an enseamed bed,
        Stewed in corruption, honeying and making love
        Over the nasty sty!

William Shakespeare   69

GERTRUDE

O, speak to me no more!
These words like daggers enter in my ears.
No more, sweet Hamlet!

HAMLET

                              A murderer and a villain,
A slave that is not twentieth part the tithe
Of your precedent lord; a vice of kings,
That from a shelf the precious diadem stole
And put it in his pocket -

GERTRUDE

No more!

HAMLET

A king of shreds and patches -

The Ghost appears.

HAMLET

Save me and hover o'er me with your wings,
You heavenly guards! - What would your gracious
     figure?

GERTRUDE

Alas, he's mad.

HAMLET

Do you not come your tardy son to chide,
That, lapsed in time and passion, lets go by
Th' important acting of your dread command?
O, say!

GHOST

    Do not forget. This visitation
    Is but to whet thy almost blunted purpose.
    But look, amazement on thy mother sits.
    Speak to her, Hamlet.

HAMLET

                    How is it with you, lady?

GERTRUDE

    Alas, how is 't with you,
    That you do bend your eye on vacancy
    And with th' incorporal air do hold discourse?
    Upon the heat and flame of thy distemper
    Sprinkle cool patience! Whereon do you look?

HAMLET

    On him, on him! Look you how pale he glares.
    Do you see nothing there?

GERTRUDE

    Nothing at all; yet all that is I see.

HAMLET

    Nor did you nothing hear?

GERTRUDE

    No, nothing but ourselves.

HAMLET

    Why, look you there, look how it steals away!
    My father, in his habit as he lived!
    Look where he goes even now out at the portal!

                    The Ghost vanishes

William Shakespeare   71

GERTRUDE

>This is the very coinage of your brain.
>This bodiless creation ecstasy
>Is very cunning in.

HAMLET

>Ecstasy?
>My pulse as yours doth temperately keep time
>And makes as healthful music. It is not madness
>That I have uttered. Mother, for love of grace,
>Lay not that flattering unction to your soul
>That not your trespass but my madness speaks,
>Infects unseen. Confess yourself to heaven,
>Repent what's past, avoid what is to come,
>And do not spread the compost on the weeds
>To make them ranker. Forgive me this my virtue,
>For, in the fatness of these pursy times,
>Virtue itself of vice must pardon beg.

GERTRUDE

>O Hamlet, thou hast cleft my heart in twain!

HAMLET

>O, throw away the worser part of it,
>And live the purer with the other half!
>Good night. But go not to my uncle's bed.
>Assume a virtue if you have it not.
>And, when you are desirous to be blest,
>I'll blessing beg of you. For this woman
>I do repent; but heaven hath pleased it so
>To punish me with this and this with me,
>That I must be their scourge and minister.
>I must be cruel only to be kind.
>This bad begins, and worse remains behind.
>I must to England, you know that.

GERTRUDE

                                  Alack,
I had forgot! 'Tis so concluded on.

HAMLET
    This one shall set me packing.
    I'll lug the guts into the neighbor room.
    Mother, good night indeed. This counselor
    Is now most still, most secret, and most grave,
    Who was in life a foolish prating knave.
    Come then, to draw toward an end with you.
    Good night, mother.

BLACKOUT

ACT TWO

SCENE ONE
the stairs

Hamlet is alone with Polonius' corpse

HAMLET
>To be or not to be - that is the question:
>Whether 'tis nobler in the mind to suffer
>The slings and arrows of outrageous fortune,
>Or to take arms against a sea of troubles
>And, by opposing, end them. To die, to sleep -
>No more - and by a sleep to say we end
>The heartache and the thousand natural shocks
>That flesh is heir to - 'tis a consummation
>Devoutly to be wished. To die, to sleep -
>To sleep, perchance to dream. Ay, there's the rub,
>For in that sleep of death what dreams may come,
>When we have shuffled off this mortal coil,
>Must give us pause. There's the respect
>That makes calamity of so long life.
>For who would bear the whips and scorns of time,
>Th' oppressor's wrong, the proud man's contumely,
>The pangs of despised love, the law's delay,
>The insolence of office, and the spurns
>That patient merit of th' unworthy takes,
>When he himself might his quietus make
>With a bare bodkin? Who would fardels bear,
>To grunt and sweat under a weary life,
>But that the dread of something after death,
>The undiscovered country from whose bourn
>No traveler returns, puzzles the will
>And makes us rather bear those ills we have
>Than fly to others that we know not of?
>Thus conscience does make cowards of us all,
>And thus the native hue of resolution

William Shakespeare

Is sicklied o'er with the pale cast of thought,
And enterprises of great pitch and moment
With this regard their currents turn awry
And lose the name of action.

SCENE TWO

the throne room

GERTRUDE

>Ah, mine own lord, what have I seen tonight!

CLAUDIUS

>What, Gertrude? How does Hamlet?

GERTRUDE

>Mad as the sea and wind when both contend
>Which is the mightier. In his lawless fit,
>Behind the arras hearing something stir,
>Whips out his father's knife, cries "A rat, a rat,"
>And in this brainish apprehension kills
>The unseen good woman.

CLAUDIUS

>O heavy deed!
>His liberty is full of threats to all -
>To you yourself, to us, to everyone.
>Alas, how shall this bloody deed be answered?
>It will be laid to us. Where is he gone?

GERTRUDE

>To draw apart the body he hath killed.

CLAUDIUS

>The sun no sooner shall the mountains touch
>But we will ship him hence; and this vile deed
>We must with all our majesty and skill
>Both countenance and excuse. Ho, Guildenstern!
>(*enter Rosencrantz and Guildenstern*)
>Hamlet in madness hath Polonius slain,
>And from his mother's closet hath he dragged him.

Go seek him out, speak fair, and bring the body
Into the chapel. I pray you, haste in this.
          (*exit Rosencrantz and Guildenstern*)
Come, Gertrude, we'll call up our wisest friends
And let them know both what we mean to do
And what's untimely done. O, come away!
My soul is full of discord and dismay.

                          HAMLET, PRINCE OF DENMARK

SCENE THREE
the courtyard

Hamlet is alone. Enter Rosencrantz and Guildenstern.

ROSENCRANTZ
> What have you done, my lord, with the dead body?

HAMLET
> Compounded it with dust, whereto 'tis kin.

ROSENCRANTZ
> Tell us where 'tis, that we may take it thence
> And bear it to the chapel.

HAMLET
> Do not believe it.

ROSENCRANTZ
> Believe what?

HAMLET
> That I can keep your counsel and not mine own.
> Besides, to be demanded of a sponge, what
> replication should be made by the son of a king?

ROSENCRANTZ
> Take you me for a sponge, my lord?

HAMLET
> Ay, sir, that soaks up the King's countenance, his
> rewards, his authorities. But such officers do the
> King best service in the end.

ROSENCRANTZ

>My lord, you must tell us where the body is and go
>with us to the King.

HAMLET

>The body is with the King, but the King is not with
>the body. The King is a thing-

GUILDENSTERN

>A "thing," my lord?

HAMLET

>Of nothing. Bring me to him.

<h1 style="text-align:center">SCENE FOUR</h1>

the throne room

ROSENCRANTZ
Where the dead body is bestowed, my lord,
We cannot get from him.

CLAUDIUS
But where is he?

ROSENCRANTZ
Without, my lord; guarded, to know your pleasure.

CLAUDIUS
Bring him before us.

ROSENCRANTZ
Ho! Bring in the lord.

Enter Guildenstern with Hamlet in handcuffs

CLAUDIUS
Now, Hamlet, where's Polonius?

HAMLET
At supper.

CLAUDIUS
At supper where?

HAMLET
>Not where she eats, but where she is eaten. A man
>may fish with the worm that hath eat of a king and
>eat of the fish that hath fed of that worm.

CLAUDIUS
>What dost thou mean by this?

HAMLET
>Nothing but to show you how a king may go a
>progress through the guts of a beggar.

CLAUDIUS
>Where is Polonius?

HAMLET
>In heaven. Send thither to see. If your messenger
>find her not there, seek her i' th' other place
>yourself. But if, indeed, you find her not within this
>month, you shall nose her as you go up the stairs
>into the lobby.

CLAUDIUS
>Go, seek her there.

Exit Guildenstern

HAMLET
>She will stay till you come.

CLAUDIUS
>Hamlet, this deed, for thine especial safety
>(Which we do tender, as we dearly grieve

For that which thou hast done) must send thee
    hence
With fiery quickness. Therefore prepare thyself.
The bark is ready, and the wind at help,
Th' associates tend, and everything is bent
For England.

HAMLET
    For England?

CLAUDIUS
    Ay, Hamlet.

HAMLET
    Good.

CLAUDIUS
    So is it, if thou knew'st our purposes.

HAMLET
    I see a cherub that sees them. But come, for
        England.
    Farewell, dear mother.

CLAUDIUS
                                    Thy loving father, Hamlet.

HAMLET
    My mother. Father and mother is man and wife,
    Man and wife is one flesh, and so, my mother. -
    Come, for England.

                    Exit Hamlet and Rosencrantz

CLAUDIUS
> And England, if my love thou hold'st at aught,
> As my great power thereof may give thee sense,
> Pays homage to us, thou mayst not coldly set
> Our sovereign process, which imports at full,
> By letters congruing to that effect,
> The present death of Hamlet. Do it, England,
> For like the hectic in my blood he rages,
> And thou must cure me. Till I know 'tis done,
> Howe'er my haps, my joys will ne'er begin.

SCENE FIVE

the seashore

ROSENCRANTZ
>Will 't please you go, my lord?

HAMLET
>I'll be with you straight. Go a little before.
>>*(exit Rosencrantz)*
>How all occasions do inform against me
>And spur my dull revenge. I do not know
>Why yet I live to say "This thing's to do,"
>Sith I have cause, and will, and strength, and means
>To do 't. How stand I, then,
>That have a father killed, a mother stained,
>Excitements of my reason and my blood,
>And let all sleep. O, from this time forth
>My thoughts be bloody or be nothing worth!

>>*Rosencrantz and Guildenstern enter. After
>>a moment Hamlet follows them off.*

SCENE SIX

the throne room

GERTRUDE

    I will not speak with her.

HORATIO

    She is importunate,
    Indeed distract; her mood will needs be pitied.

GERTRUDE

    What would she have?

HORATIO

    She speaks much of her father, says she hears
    There's tricks i' th' world, and hems, and beats her
        heart.
    'Twere good she were spoken with, for she may
        strew
    Dangerous conjectures in ill-breeding minds.

GERTRUDE

    Let her come in.

Enter Ophelia

OPHELIA

    Where is the beauteous Majesty of Denmark?

GERTRUDE

    How now, Ophelia?

OPHELIA

       (sings)
    How should I your true love know
      From another one?

GERTRUDE

    Alas, sweet lady, what imports this song?

OPHELIA

    Say you? Nay, pray you, mark.
        (Sings)
    He is dead and gone, lady,
      He is dead and gone;
    At his head a grass-green turf,
      At his heels a stone.

    Oh, ho!

GERTRUDE

    Nay, but Ophelia -

        Enter Claudius

OPHELIA

    Pray you, mark.
        (sings)
    White his shroud as the mountain snow-
      Larded all with sweet flowers;
    Which bewept to the ground did not go
      With true-love showers.

William Shakespeare

CLAUDIUS
> How do you, pretty lady?

OPHELIA
> They say the owl was a baker's daughter. Lord, we
> know what we are but know not what we may be.
> Pray let's have no words of this, but when they ask
> you what it means, say you this:
>> (sings)
> Tomorrow is Saint Valentine's day,
>> All in the morning betime,
> And I a maid at your window,
>> To be your Valentine.
> Then up he rose and donned his clothes
>> And dupped the chamber door,
> Let in the maid, that out a maid
>> Never departed more.

CLAUDIUS
> Pretty Ophelia -

OPHELIA
> Indeed, without an oath, I'll make an end on 't:
>> (sings)
> By Gis and by Saint Charity,
>> Alack and fie for shame,
> Young men will do 't, if they come to 't;
>> By Cock, they are to blame.
> Quoth she "Before you tumbled me,
>> You promised me to wed."

> He answers:

>> "So would I 'a done, by yonder sun,
>>> An thou hadst not come to my bed."

                    HAMLET, PRINCE OF DENMARK

CLAUDIUS

> How long hath she been thus?

OPHELIA

> I hope all will be well. We must be patient, but I
> cannot choose but weep to think they would lay
> him i' th' cold ground. My brother shall know of it.
> And so I thank you for your good counsel. Good
> night, ladies, good night, sweet ladies, good night,
> good night.
> > (*exits*)

CLAUDIUS

> Follow her close; give her good watch, I pray you.
> > (*exit Horatio*)
> O, this is the poison of deep grief. It springs
> All from her father's death, and now behold!
> When sorrows come, they come not single spies,
> But in battalions: first, her father slain;
> Next, your son gone, and he most violent author
> Of his own just remove; poor Ophelia
> Divided from herself and her fair judgment.
> Last, and as much containing as all these,
> Her brother is in secret come from France.

GERTRUDE

> Alack, what noise is this?

Enter Laertes

LAERTES

> Where is this king? O, thou vile king,
> Give me my mother!

GERTRUDE

> Calmly, good Laertes.

LAERTES

That drop of blood that's calm proclaims me
    bastard,
Cries "cuckold" to my father, brands the harlot
Even here between the chaste unsmirched brow
Of my true mother.

CLAUDIUS

> What is the cause, Laertes,
That thy rebellion looks so giant-like?
Let him go, Gertrude. Do not fear our person.
Why art thou thus incensed. Let him go, Gertrude.
Speak, man.

LAERTES

Where is my father?

CLAUDIUS

Dead.

GERTRUDE

But not by him.

CLAUDIUS

> Let him demand his fill.

LAERTES

How came he dead? I'll not be juggled with.
To hell, allegiance! Vows, to the blackest devil!
I dare damnation. To this point I stand,
That both the worlds I give to negligence,
Let come what comes, only I'll be revenged
Most throughly for my mother.

CLAUDIUS
    Who shall stay you?

LAERTES
    My will, not all the world.
    And for my means, I'll husband them so well
    They shall go far with little.

CLAUDIUS
                        Good Laertes,
    If you desire to know the certainty
    Of your dear mother, is 't writ in your revenge
    That, swoopstake, you will draw both friend and
        foe,
    Winner and loser?

LAERTES
    None but her enemies.

CLAUDIUS
    Will you know them, then?

LAERTES
    To her good friends thus wide I'll ope my arms
    And, like the kind life-rend'ring pelican,
    Repast them with my blood.

CLAUDIUS
    That I am guiltless of your mother's death
    And am most sensibly in grief for it,
    It shall as level to your judgment 'pear
    As day does to your eye.

LAERTES
    How now, what noise is that?
            (*Ophelia enters*)

William Shakespeare   93

LAERTES

Dear maid, kind sister, sweet Ophelia!
O heavens, is 't possible a young maid's wits
Should be as mortal as an old man's life?

OPHELIA

  (sings)
They bore him barefaced on the bier,
 Hey non nonny, nonny, hey nonny,
And in his grave rained many a tear.

Fare you well, my dove.

LAERTES

Hadst thou thy wits and didst persuade revenge,
It could not move thus.

OPHELIA

There's rosemary, that's for remembrance. Pray
you, love, remember. And there is pansies, that's
for thoughts.

LAERTES

A document in madness: thoughts and
remembrance fitted.

OPHELIA

There's fennel for you, and columbines. There's rue
for you, and here's some for me; we may call it herb
of grace o' Sundays. You must wear your rue with a
difference. There's a daisy. I would give you some
violets, but they withered all when my father died.
  (sings)
For bonny sweet Robin is all my joy.

LAERTES

> Thought and afflictions, passion, hell itself
> She turns to favor and to prettiness.

OPHELIA

> (*sings*)
> *And will she not come again?*
> *And will she not come again?*
> *No, no, she is dead.*
> *Go to thy deathbed.*
> *She never will come again.*

> God 'a mercy on her soul. And of all Christians'
> souls, I pray God. God be wi' you.
> (*exits*)

LAERTES

> Do you see this, O God?

CLAUDIUS

> Laertes, I must commune with your grief.
> Make choice of whom your wisest friends you will,
> And they shall hear and judge 'twixt you and me.
> If by direct or by collateral hand
> They find us touched, we will our kingdom give,
> Our crown, our life, and all that we call ours,
> To you in satisfaction; but if not,
> Be you content to lend your patience to us,
> And we shall jointly labor with your soul
> To give it due content.

LAERTES

>   Let this be so.
> Her means of death, her obscure funeral,
> That I must call 't in question.

CLAUDIUS

                              So you shall,
          And where th' offense is, let the great ax fall.
          I pray you, go with me.

SCENE SEVEN
the courtyard

HORATIO

       (*reading*)
"Horatio,

Ere we were two days old at sea, a pirate of very warlike appointment gave us chase. Finding ourselves too slow of sail, we put on a compelled valor, and in the grapple I boarded them. On the instant, they got clear of our ship; so I alone became their prisoner. They have dealt with me like thieves of mercy, but they knew what they did. Let the King have the letters I have sent, and repair thou to me with as much speed as thou wouldst fly death. Rosencrantz and Guildenstern hold their course for England. Farewell.

      He that thou knowest thine,

      Hamlet"

SCENE EIGHT
the throne room

CLAUDIUS

> Now must your conscience my acquittance seal,
> And you must put me in your heart for friend,
> Sith you have heard, and with a knowing ear,
> That he which hath your noble father slain
> Pursued my life.

LAERTES

> But my revenge will come.
> And so have I a noble father lost,
> And sister driven into desp'rate terms.

CLAUDIUS

> Break not your sleeps for that. You must not think
> That we are made of stuff so flat and dull
> That we can let our beard be shook with danger
> And think it pastime. You shortly shall hear more.
> I loved your father, and we love ourself,
> And that, I hope, will teach you to imagine -

Enter Horatio

CLAUDIUS

> How now? What news?

HORATIO

> Letters, my lord, from Hamlet.
> These to your Majesty, this to the Queen.

CLAUDIUS

> From Hamlet? Who brought them?

                    HAMLET, PRINCE OF DENMARK

HORATIO

Sailors, my lord, they say. I saw them not.

CLAUDIUS

Laertes, you shall hear them. Leave us.

Horatio exits.

CLAUDIUS

(*reads*)
"High and mighty,

You shall know I am set naked on your kingdom.
Tomorrow shall I beg leave to see your kingly eyes,
when I shall, first asking your pardon, thereunto
recount the occasion of my sudden and more
strange return.
Hamlet"

What should this mean? Are all the rest come back?
Or is it some abuse and no such thing?

LAERTES

Know you the hand?

CLAUDIUS

'Tis Hamlet's character. "Naked"
And in a postscript here, he says "alone."
Can you advise me?

LAERTES

I am lost in it, my lord. But let him come.
It warms the very sickness in my heart

William Shakespeare   99

That I shall live and tell him to his teeth
"Thus didst thou."

CLAUDIUS

            If it be so, Laertes
Will you be ruled by me?

LAERTES

                Ay, my lord,
So you will not o'errule me to a peace.

CLAUDIUS
    To thine own peace. If he be now returned,
    As checking at his voyage, and that he means
    No more to undertake it, I will work him
    To an exploit, now ripe in my device,
    Under the which he shall not choose but fall;
    And for his death no wind of blame shall breathe,
    But even his mother shall uncharge the practice
    And call it accident.

LAERTES
          My lord, I will be ruled,
The rather if you could devise it so
That I might be the organ.

CLAUDIUS
              It falls right.
Laertes, was your father dear to you?
Or are you like the painting of a sorrow,
A face without a heart?

LAERTES

           Why ask you this?

CLAUDIUS

Not that I think you did not love your father,
But that I know love is begun by time
And that I see, in passages of proof,
Time qualifies the spark and fire of it.
Hamlet comes back; what would you undertake
To show yourself indeed your father's son
More than in words?

LAERTES

To cut his throat i' th' church.

CLAUDIUS

No place indeed should murder sanctuarize;
Revenge should have no bounds. But, good
    Laertes,
Will you do this? Keep close within your chamber.
Hamlet, returned, shall know you are come home.
We'll put on those shall praise your excellence
And wager on your heads. He, being remiss,
Most generous, and free from all contriving,
Will not peruse the foils, so that with ease,
Or with a little shuffling, you may choose
A sword unbated, and in a pass of practice
Requite him for your father.

LAERTES

I will do 't,
I bought an unction of a mountebank
So mortal that, but dip a knife in it,
Where it draws blood no cataplasm so rare
Under the moon, can save the thing from death
That is but scratched withal. I'll touch my point
With this contagion, that, if I gall him slightly,
It may be death.

CLAUDIUS

                        Let's further think of this,
Weigh what convenience both of time and means
May fit us to our shape. If this should fail,
And that our drift look through our bad
    performance,
'Twere better not assayed. Soft, let me see.
We'll make a solemn wager on your cunnings -
I ha 't!
When in your motion you are hot and dry
And that he calls for drink, I'll have prepared him
A chalice for the nonce, whereon but sipping,
Our purpose may hold there. - But stay, what
    noise?

Enter Gertrude

GERTRUDE

One woe doth tread upon another's heel,
So fast they follow. Your sister's drowned, Laertes.

LAERTES

Drowned? O, where?

GERTRUDE

There is a willow grows askant the brook
That shows his hoar leaves in the glassy stream.
Therewith fantastic garlands did she make
Of crowflowers, nettles, daisies, and long purples,
That liberal shepherds give a grosser name,
But our cold maids do "dead men's fingers" call
    them.
There on the pendant boughs her coronet weeds

Clamb'ring to hang, an envious sliver broke,
When down her weedy trophies and herself
Fell in the weeping brook. Her clothes spread wide,
And mermaid-like awhile they bore her up,
Which time she chanted snatches of old lauds,
As one incapable of her own distress
Or like a creature native and endued
Unto that element. But long it could not be
Till that her garments, heavy with their drink,
Pulled the poor wretch from her melodious lay
To muddy death.

LAERTES

Alas, then she is drowned.

GERTRUDE
Drowned, drowned.

LAERTES
Too much of water hast thou, poor Ophelia,
And therefore I forbid my tears. But yet
It is our trick; nature her custom holds,
Let shame say what it will. When these are gone,
The woman will be out. - Adieu, my lord.
I have a speech o' fire that fain would blaze,
But that this folly drowns it.
(exits)

CLAUDIUS

Let's follow, Gertrude.
How much I had to do to calm his rage!
Now fear I this will give it start again.
Therefore, let's follow.

SCENE NINE

the graveyard

GRAVEDIGGER

>What is he that builds stronger than either the
>mason, the shipwright, or the carpenter? The
>gallows-maker; for that frame outlives a thousand
>tenants. Who builds stronger than a mason, a
>shipwright, or a carpenter? A grave-maker! The
>houses he makes lasts till doomsday.

Enter Hamlet and Horatio

HAMLET

>You do remember all the circumstance?

HORATIO

>Remember it, my lord!

HAMLET

>Sir, in my heart there was a kind of fighting
>That would not let me sleep. That should learn us
>There's a divinity that shapes our ends,
>Rough-hew them how we will -

HORATIO

>   That is most certain.

HAMLET

>Up from my cabin,
>Groped I to find out them; making so bold
>(My fears forgetting manners) to unfold
>Their grand commission; where I found, Horatio,
>A royal knavery - an exact command,

That on the supervise, no leisure bated,
My head should be struck off.

HORATIO

Is 't possible?

HAMLET
Here's the commission. Read it at more leisure.
(gives the papers to Horatio)
Or I could make a prologue to my brains,
They had begun the play. I sat me down,
Devised a new commission, wrote it fair-
An earnest conjuration from the King,
That, on the view and knowing of these contents,
Without debatement further, more or less,
He should those bearers put to sudden death,
Not shriving time allowed.

HORATIO

How was this sealed?

HAMLET
I had my father's signet in my purse,
Which was the model of that Danish seal.

HORATIO
So Guildenstern and Rosencrantz go to 't.

HAMLET
They are not near my conscience. Their defeat
Does by their own insinuation grow.
'Tis dangerous when the baser nature comes
Between the pass and fell incensed points
Of mighty opposites.
(the Gravedigger whistles as he digs)

Has this fellow no feeling of his business? He
whistles in grave-making.

HORATIO

Custom hath made it in him a property of easiness.

The Gravedigger digs up a skull

HAMLET

That skull had a tongue in it and could sing once.
How the knave jowls it to the ground as if 'twere
Cain's jawbone, that did the first murder! I will
speak to this fellow. - Whose grave's this, sirrah?

GRAVEDIGGER

Mine, sir.

HAMLET

I think it be thine indeed, for thou liest in 't.

GRAVEDIGGER

You lie out on 't, sir, and therefore 'tis not yours.
For my part, I do not lie in 't, yet it is mine.

HAMLET

Thou dost lie in 't, to be in 't and say it is thine. 'Tis
for the dead, not for the quick; therefore thou liest.

GRAVEDIGGER

'Tis a quick lie, sir; 'twill away again from me to you.

HAMLET

What man dost thou dig it for?

          HAMLET, PRINCE OF DENMARK

GRAVEDIGGER
    For no man, sir.

HAMLET
    What woman then?

GRAVEDIGGER
    For none, neither.

HAMLET
    Who is to be buried in 't?

GRAVEDIGGER
    One that was a woman, sir, but, rest her soul, she's
    dead.

HAMLET
    How absolute the knave is! How long hast thou
    been grave-maker?

GRAVEDIGGER
    Of all the days i' th' year, I came to 't that day that
    our last King Hamlet overcame Fortinbras.

HAMLET
    How long is that since?

GRAVEDIGGER
    Cannot you tell that? Every fool can tell that. It was
    that very day that young Hamlet was born. He that
    is mad, and sent into England.

HAMLET
    Ay, marry, why was he sent into England?

GRAVEDIGGER
    Why, because he was mad. He shall recover his wits
    there. Or if he do not, 'tis no great matter there.

HAMLET
    Why?

GRAVEDIGGER
    'Twill not be seen in him there. There the men are
    as mad as he.

HAMLET
    How came he mad?

GRAVEDIGGER
    Very strangely, they say.

HAMLET
    How "strangely"?

GRAVEDIGGER
    Faith, e'en with losing his wits.

HAMLET
    Upon what ground?

GRAVEDIGGER
    Why, here in Denmark. I have been sexton here
    thirty years.

HAMLET
    How long will a man lie i' th' earth ere he rot?

GRAVEDIGGER
    Faith, if he be not rotten before he die (as we have
    many pocky corses nowadays that will scarce hold

                    HAMLET, PRINCE OF DENMARK

the laying in), he will last you some eight year or
nine year. Here's a skull now hath lien you i' th'
earth three-and-twenty years.

HAMLET
Whose was it?

GRAVEDIGGER
A whoreson mad fellow's it was. Whose do you
think it was?

HAMLET
Nay, I know not.

GRAVEDIGGER
A pestilence on him for a mad rogue! He poured a
flagon of Rhenish on my head once. This same
skull, sir, was, sir, Yorick's skull, the King's jester.

HAMLET
This?

GRAVEDIGGER
E'en that.

HAMLET
Let me see. Alas, poor Yorick! I knew him, Horatio.
He hath bore me on his back a thousand times, and
now how abhorred in my imagination it is! Here
hung those lips that I have kissed I know not how
oft. Where be your gibes now? Your flashes of
merriment that were wont to set the table on a
roar? Not one now to mock your own grinning?
Now get you to my lady's chamber, and tell her, let
her paint an inch thick. Make her laugh at that.
(*a noise offstage*)

William Shakespeare   109

But soft, but soft awhile! Here comes the King, The
Queen, the courtiers. Who is this they follow?

*Exit the Gravedigger. Enter King, Queen,
Laertes, and the corpse of Ophelia.
Hamlet and Horatio hide themselves.*

LAERTES

Must there no more be done?

GERTRUDE

No more be done.
We should profane the service of the dead
To sing a requiem and such rest to her
As to peace-parted souls.

LAERTES

Lay her i' th' earth,
And from her fair and unpolluted flesh
May violets spring!

HAMLET

(to Horatio)
What, the fair Ophelia?

GERTRUDE

Sweets to the sweet, farewell!
I hoped thou shouldst have been my Hamlet's wife;
I thought thy bride-bed to have decked, sweet
    maid,
And not have strewed thy grave.

LAERTES

O, treble woe

    HAMLET, PRINCE OF DENMARK

Fall ten times treble on that cursed head
Whose wicked deed thy most ingenious sense
Deprived thee of! - Hold off the earth awhile,
Till I have caught her once more in mine arms.

HAMLET
          (*revealing himself*)
I loved Ophelia. Forty thousand brothers
Could not with all their quantity of love
Make up my sum. What wilt thou do for her?

Laertes attacks Hamlet

CLAUDIUS
     O, he is mad, Laertes!

GERTRUDE
     For love of God, forbear him.

HAMLET
     I prithee, take thy fingers from my throat;
     For, though I am not splenitive and rash,
     Yet have I something in me dangerous,
     Which let thy wiseness fear: hold off thy hand.

CLAUDIUS
     Pluck them asunder.

GERTRUDE
     Hamlet, Hamlet!

CLAUDIUS
     Gentlemen!

HORATIO
>Good my lord, be quiet.
>>*(pulls Hamlet away from Laertes)*

HAMLET
>'Swounds, show me what thou 't do.
>Woo't weep, woo't fight, woo't fast, woo't tear
>>thyself,
>I'll do 't. Dost thou come here to whine?
>To outface me with leaping in her grave?
>Be buried quick with her, and so will I.
>I'll rant as well as thou.

GERTRUDE
>>This is mere madness;
>And thus awhile the fit will work on him.

HAMLET
>What is the reason that you use me thus?
>I loved you ever. But it is no matter.
>Let Hercules himself do what he may,
>The cat will mew, and dog will have his day.
>>*(exits)*

CLAUDIUS
>I pray thee, good Horatio, wait upon him.
>>*(exit Horatio)*
>Strengthen your patience in our last night's speech.
>We'll put the matter to the present push.
>Good Gertrude, set some watch over your son.
>>*(exit Gertrude)*
>This grave shall have a living monument.
>An hour of quiet thereby shall we see.
>Till then in patience our proceeding be.

　　　　HAMLET, PRINCE OF DENMARK

SCENE TEN

the throne room

HAMLET

So much for this, sir. Now shall you see the other.
Does it not, think thee, stand me now upon-
He that hath killed my king and whored my mother,
Thrown out his angle for my proper life,
And with such cozenage - is 't not perfect
conscience
To quit him with this arm?

HORATIO

It must be shortly known to him from England
What is the issue of the business there.

HAMLET

It will be short. The interim's mine,
And a man's life's no more than to say "one."
But I am very sorry, good Horatio,
That to Laertes I forgot myself.

HORATIO

The King, sir, hath laid, that in a dozen passes
between yourself and him, he shall not exceed you
three hits.

HAMLET

If it please his Majesty, it is the breathing time of
day with me. Let the foils be brought, the
gentleman willing, and the King hold his purpose.

*Horatio exits and returns with Hamlet's
foil and mask.*

William Shakespeare   113

HORATIO

The Queen desires you to use some gentle
entertainment to Laertes before you fall to play.

HAMLET

She well instructs me.

HORATIO

You will lose, my lord.

HAMLET

I do not think so. Since he went into France, I have
been in continual practice. I shall win at the odds.

HORATIO

If your mind dislike anything, obey it. I will forestall
their repair hither and say you are not fit.

HAMLET

Not a whit. We defy augury. There is a special
providence in the fall of a sparrow. If it be now, 'tis
not to come; if it be not to come, it will be now; if it
be not now, yet it will come. The readiness is all.
Since no man of aught he leaves knows, what is 't
to leave betimes? Let be.

Enter Gertrude, Laertes, and Claudius.

CLAUDIUS

Come, Hamlet, come and take this hand from me.

HAMLET

(to Laertes)
Give me your pardon, sir. I have done you wrong.

Was 't Hamlet wronged Laertes? Never Hamlet.
Who does it, then? His madness. If 't be so,
His madness is poor Hamlet's enemy.
Sir, in this audience
Let my disclaiming from a purposed evil
Free me so far in your most generous thoughts
That I have shot my arrow o'er the house
And hurt my brother.

LAERTES
I am satisfied in nature,
Whose motive in this case should stir me most
To my revenge; but in my terms of honor
I stand aloof and will no reconcilement
Till by some elder masters of known honor
I have a voice and precedent of peace
To keep my name ungored. But till that time
I do receive your offered love like love
And will not wrong it.

HAMLET
                              I embrace it freely
And will this brothers' wager frankly play.
Give us the foils. Come on.

LAERTES
                              Come, one for me.

HAMLET
I'll be your foil, Laertes; in mine ignorance
Your skill shall, like a star i' th' darkest night,
Stick fiery off indeed.

LAERTES
                    You mock me, sir.

HAMLET
   No, by this hand.

CLAUDIUS
   Give them the foils, Horatio. Cousin Hamlet,
   You know the wager?

HAMLET
                         Very well, my lord.
   Your Grace has laid the odds o' th' weaker side.

CLAUDIUS
   I do not fear it; I have seen you both.
   But, since he is better, we have therefore odds.

LAERTES
   This is too heavy. Let me see another.

HAMLET
   This likes me well. These foils have all a length?

LAERTES
   Ay, my good lord.

CLAUDIUS
   If Hamlet give the first or second hit
   Or quit in answer of the third exchange,
   The King shall drink to Hamlet's better breath,
   And in the cup an union shall he throw.
   Now the King drinks to Hamlet. Come, begin.

HAMLET
   Come on, sir.

LAERTES
   Come, my lord.

                    HAMLET, PRINCE OF DENMARK

Hamlet and Laertes fight. Hamlet scores the first hit.

HAMLET
One.

LAERTES
No.

HAMLET
Judgment!

CLAUDIUS
A hit, a very palpable hit.

LAERTES
Well, again.

CLAUDIUS
Stay, give me drink. - Hamlet, this pearl is thine. Here's to thy health.

Claudius drinks, then drops the pearl into the cup.

CLAUDIUS
Give him the cup.

HAMLET
I'll play this bout first. Set it by awhile. Come.

Hamlet and Laertes fight. Hamlet scores again.

HAMLET

Another hit. What say you?

LAERTES

A touch, a touch. I do confess 't.

CLAUDIUS

Our son shall win.

GERTRUDE

He's fat and scant of breath.
The Queen carouses to thy fortune, Hamlet.
(lifts the cup)

HAMLET

Good madam.

CLAUDIUS

Gertrude, do not drink.

GERTRUDE

I will, my lord; I pray you pardon me.
(drinks)

CLAUDIUS

(aside) It is the poisoned cup. It is too late.

HAMLET

I dare not drink yet, madam - by and by.

GERTRUDE

Come, let me wipe thy face.

          HAMLET, PRINCE OF DENMARK

LAERTES
My lord, I'll hit him now.

CLAUDIUS
I do not think 't.

LAERTES
(*aside*) And yet it is almost against my conscience.

HAMLET
Come, for the third, Laertes. You do but dally.
I pray you pass with your best violence.
I am afeard you make a wanton of me.

LAERTES
Say you so? Come on.

Hamlet and Laertes fight to a standstill

HORATIO
Nothing neither way.

LAERTES
Have at you now!

*Laertes wounds Hamlet from behind.
Then in scuffling they change swords, and
Hamlet wounds Laertes.*

CLAUDIUS
Part them. They are incensed.

William Shakespeare

HAMLET

> Nay, come again.
>> (*Gertrude falls*)
> Look to the Queen there, ho!

HORATIO

> They bleed on both sides. How is it, my lord?

CLAUDIUS

> How is 't, Laertes?

LAERTES

> I am justly killed with mine own treachery.

HAMLET

> How does the Queen?

CLAUDIUS

>> She swoons to see them bleed.

GERTRUDE

> No, no, the drink, the drink! O, my dear Hamlet!
> The drink, the drink! I am poisoned.
>> (*dies*)

HAMLET

> O villainy! Ho! Let the door be locked.
> Treachery! Seek it out.

LAERTES

> It is here, Hamlet. Hamlet, thou art slain.
> No med'cine in the world can do thee good.
> In thee there is not half an hour's life.
> The treacherous instrument is in thy hand,
> Unbated and envenomed. The foul practice
> Hath turned itself on me. Lo, here I lie,

　　　　　　　HAMLET, PRINCE OF DENMARK

Never to rise again. Thy mother's poisoned.
I can no more. The King, the King's to blame.

HAMLET
The point envenomed too! Then, venom, to thy
work.

*Hamlet stabs Claudius, tosses the foil
aside and picks up the cup.*

CLAUDIUS
Treason, treason!
O, yet defend me, friends! I am but hurt.

HAMLET
Here, thou incestuous, murd'rous, damned Dane,
Drink off this potion. Is thy union here?
Follow my mother.

*Hamlet forcefully pours the poisoned
wine down Claudius' throat. He dies.*

LAERTES
He is justly served.
It is a poison tempered by himself.
Exchange forgiveness with me, noble Hamlet.
Mine and my father's death come not upon thee,
Nor thine on me.
(*dies*)

HAMLET
Heaven make thee free of it. I follow thee.

I am dead, Horatio. Wretched queen, adieu.
You that look pale and tremble at this chance,
That are but mutes or audience to this act,
Had I but time (as this fell sergeant, Death,
Is strict in his arrest), O, I could tell you -
But let it be. - Horatio, I am dead.
Thou livest; report me and my cause aright
To the unsatisfied.

HORATIO

                      Never believe it.
I am more an antique Roman than a Dane.
Here's yet some liquor left.
              (picks up the cup)

HAMLET

                          As thou 'rt a man,
Give me the cup. Let go! By heaven, I'll ha 't.
          (takes the cup and drinks)
O God, Horatio, what a wounded name,
Things standing thus unknown, shall I leave behind
   me!
If thou didst ever hold me in thy heart,
Absent thee from felicity awhile
And in this harsh world draw thy breath in pain
To tell my story. The rest is silence.
           (dies)

HORATIO

Now cracks a noble heart. Good night, sweet
   prince,
And flights of angels sing thee to thy rest.
And let me speak to th' yet unknowing world
How these things came about. So shall you hear
Of carnal, bloody, and unnatural acts,

Of accidental judgments, casual slaughters,
Of deaths put on by cunning and forced cause.
But let this same be presently performed
Even while men's minds are wild, lest more
    mischance
On plots and errors happen. Let four captains
Bear Hamlet like a soldier to the stage,
For he was likely, had he been put on,
To have proved most royal; and for his passage,
The soldier's music and the rite of war
Speak loudly for him.
Take up the bodies. Such a sight as this
Becomes the field but here shows much amiss.
Go, bid the soldiers shoot.

END OF PLAY

About the adaptation

I prepared this adaptation for a cast of 9 performing in a small theater. The plot was streamlined to focus on the family dynamics of the primary characters by eliminating most minor characters and the sub-plot involving Fortinbras except for a few passing references. Rosencrantz and Guildenstern have had their roles expanded by the inclusion of text originally written for the Players. While the text has been cut significantly in some places, I have made very few alterations to the remaining lines. What alterations have been made were to provide consistency with the production concept, or to fix holes in the meter left by my original cutting.

This adaptation is heavily influenced by an adaptation I prepared for a 2010 production, also from New Muses Theatre Company, at the Roxy Theater in Morton.

–Niclas Olson

About the playwright

William Shakespeare was born in 1564 and is widely regarded as the greatest writer in the history of the English language. Shakespeare's many works include *Othello; Macbeth; King Lear; Romeo and Juliet; A Midsummer Night's Dream; As You Like It; Twelfth Night; The Tempest; Richard II; Henry V;* and *Richard IIII.* Shakespeare died in 1616.

About the adaptor

Niclas Olson's adaptations of Shakespeare's *Hamlet*, *Romeo and Juliet*, Christopher Marlowe's *Doctor Faustus*, August Strindberg's *Miss Julie*, Carlo Goldoni's *A Servant of Two Masters*, Luigi Pirandello's *Six Characters in Search of an Author*, Henrik Ibsen's *Ghosts*, *A Doll's House*, and *Peer Gynt*, Anton Chekhov's *The Seagull*, Moliére's *Tartuffe*, Aristophanes' *Lysistrata* and Mary Shelley's *Frankenstein* were commissioned and performed by New Muses Theatre Company. His original plays *Last Waltz on a Midnight Violin and Dirty Laundry* have been staged at Pacific Lutheran University. He studied playwriting in London and received his degree in theatre from Pacific Lutheran University

also available from New Muses

Lysistrata by Aristophanes

The Seagull by Anton Chekhov

A Servant of Two Masters by Carlo Goldoni

A Doll's House by Henrik Ibsen

Ghosts by Henrik Ibsen

Peer Gynt by Henrik Ibsen

Doctor Faustus by Christopher Marlowe

Tartuffe by Molière

6 Characters in Search of an Author by Luigi Pirandello

Hamlet, Prince of Denmark by William Shakespeare

Romeo & Juliet by William Shakespeare

Miss Julie by August Strindberg

Riders to the Sea & In the Shadow of the Glen by J.M. Synge

The Importance of Being Earnest by Oscar Wilde

Dulcitius, The Rising of the Moon & Every Afternoon
a trinity of plays by Hrotsvitha, Lady Gregory, and Gertrude Stein

www.NewMuses.com

www.ingramcontent.com/pod-product-compliance
Lightning Source LLC
Chambersburg PA
CBHW022136150726
47992CB00002B/618